Piano • Vocal • Guitar

Love Songs of the 60's

This publication is not for sale in
the E.C. and/or Australia
or New Zealand.

ISBN 0-7935-4456-4

HAL • LEONARD
CORPORATION
7777 W. BLUEMOUND RD. P.O. BOX 13819 MILWAUKEE, WI 53213

ALL MY LOVING

Words and Music by JOHN LENN
and PAUL McCART

Brightly, with a swing feel (♩♩ played as ♩³♪)

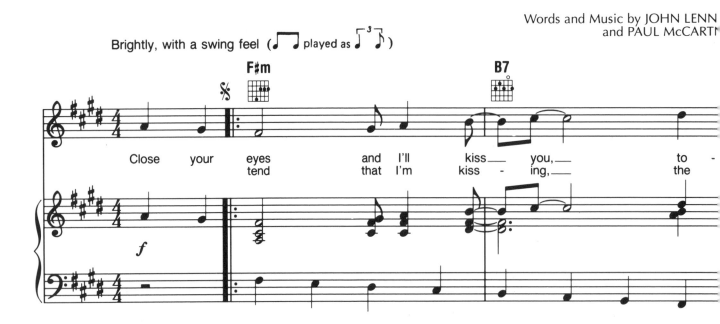

Close your eyes and I'll kiss you,
tend that I'm kiss-ing, to the

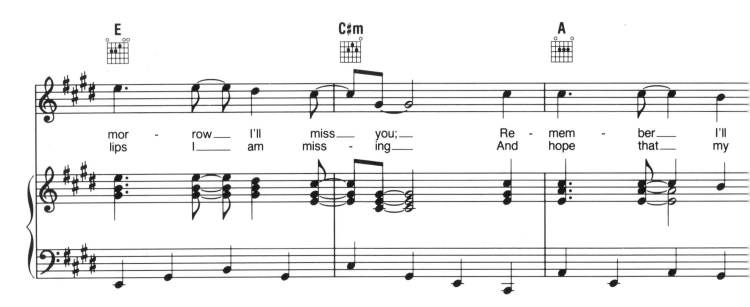

mor-row I'll miss you; Re-mem-ber I'll
lips I am miss-ing And hope that my

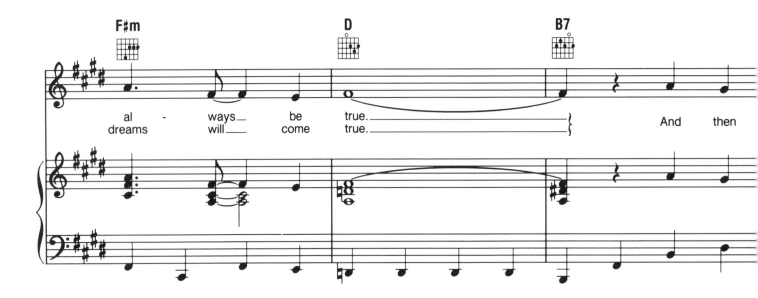

al-ways be true.
dreams will come true. And then

you, _____ All ___ my lov - ing, ___ dar -

- ling, I'll ___ be true. _____

ALL YOU NEED IS LOVE

Words and Music by JOHN LENNON
and PAUL McCARTNEY

There's noth-ing you can do that can't be done.___
There's noth-ing you can make that can't be made.___
There's noth-ing you can know that is-n't known.___

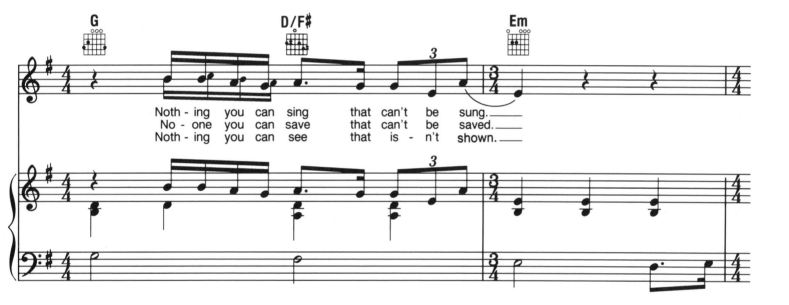

Noth-ing you can sing that can't be sung.___
No - one you can save that can't be saved.___
Noth-ing you can see that is-n't shown.___

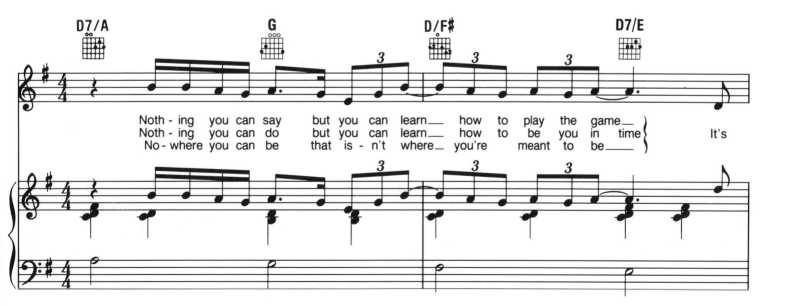

Noth-ing you can say but you can learn___ how to play the game___
Noth-ing you can do but you can learn___ how to be you in time
No - where you can be that is-n't where___ you're meant to be___

It's

9

AND I LOVE HER

Words and Music by JOHN LENNON
and PAUL McCARTNEY

12

CAN'T HELP FALLING IN LOVE

Words and Music by GEORGE DAVID WEISS,
HUGO PERETTI and LUIGI CREATORE

Moderately Slow

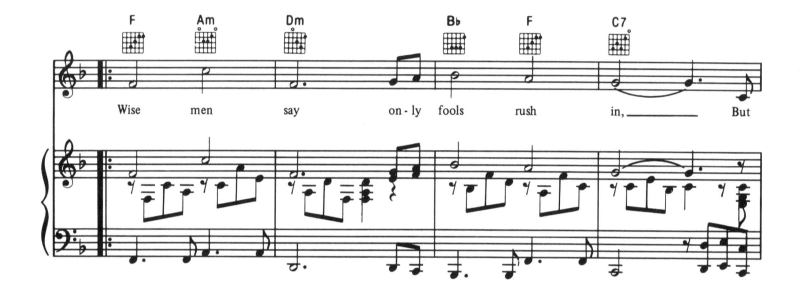

Wise men say on-ly fools rush in, _____ But

I Can't Help Fall-ing In Love with

CHERISH

Words and Music by
TERRY KIRKMAN

COME SATURDAY MORNING
(a/k/a SATURDAY MORNING)
from the Paramount Picture THE STERILE CUCKOO

Words by DORY PREVIN
Music by FRED KARLIN

Moderato but not too slow

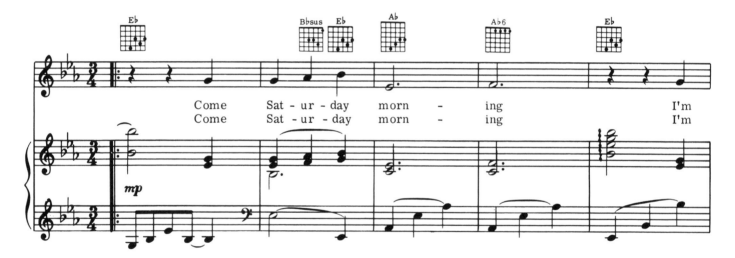

Come Sat-ur-day morn — ing I'm
Come Sat-ur-day morn — ing I'm

go - ing a - way with my friend; We'll
go - ing a - way with my friend; We'll

Sat - ur - day spend till the end of the day.
Sat - ur - day laugh more than half of the day.

Just I and my friend.
Just I and my friend.

We'll trav - el for miles in our Sat - ur - day smiles,
dressed up in our rings and our Sat - ur - day things,

and then we'll move on.

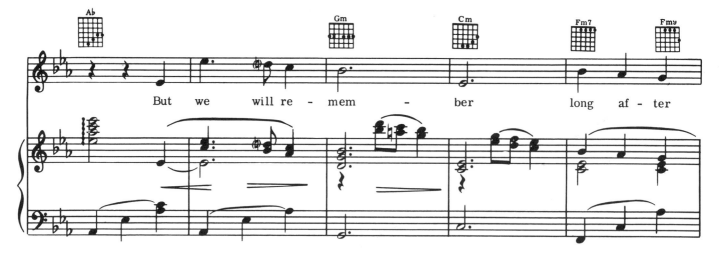

But we will re - mem - ber long af - ter

Sat - ur-day's gone. Come Sat - ur - day Morn - ing.

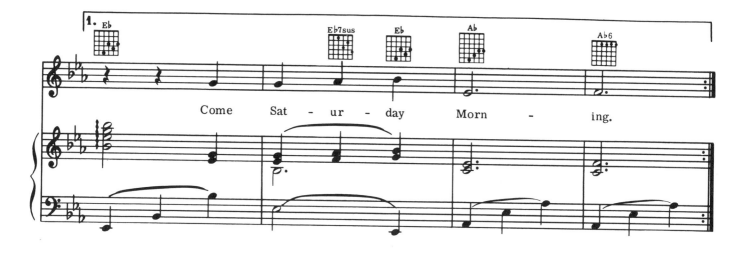

1.

Come Sat - ur - day Morn - ing.

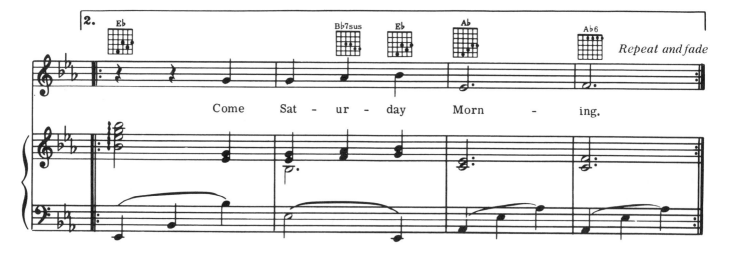

2. *Repeat and fade*

Come Sat - ur - day Morn - ing.

DEDICATED TO THE ONE I LOVE

Words and Music by LOWMAN PAULING
and RALPH BASS

A GROOVY KIND OF LOVE

Words and Music by TONI WINE
and CAROLE BAYER SAGER

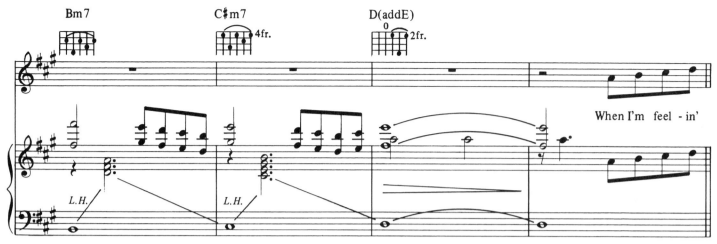

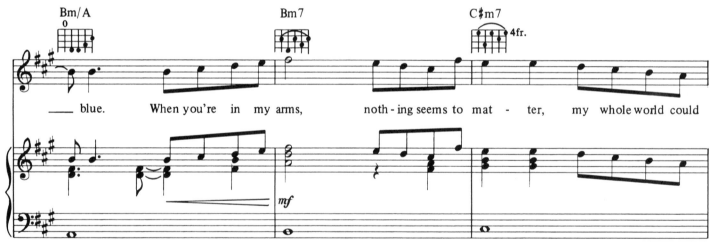

GOIN' OUT OF MY HEAD

Words and Music by TEDDY RANDAZZO
and BOBBY WEINSTEIN

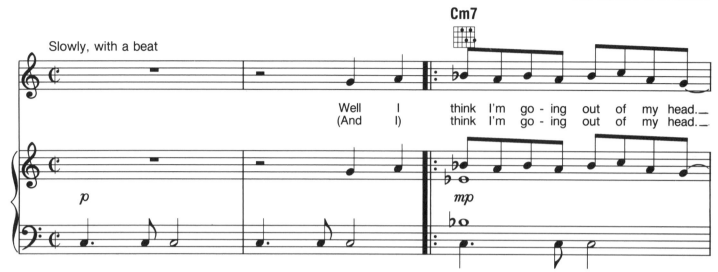

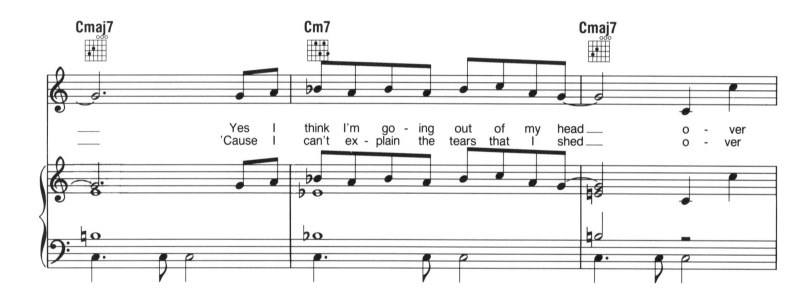

HOOKED ON A FEELING

Words and Music by
MARK JAMES

38

HERE, THERE AND EVERYWHERE

Words and Music by JOHN LENNON
and PAUL McCARTNEY

HOW INSENSITIVE
(INSENSATEZ)

Original Words by VINICIUS de MORAES
English Words by NORMAN GIMBEL
Music by ANTONIO CARLOS JOBIM

MCA music publishing

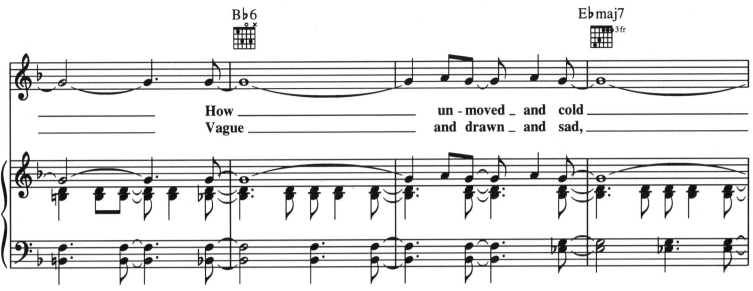

How _____ un-moved _ and cold _____
Vague _____ and drawn _ and sad, _____

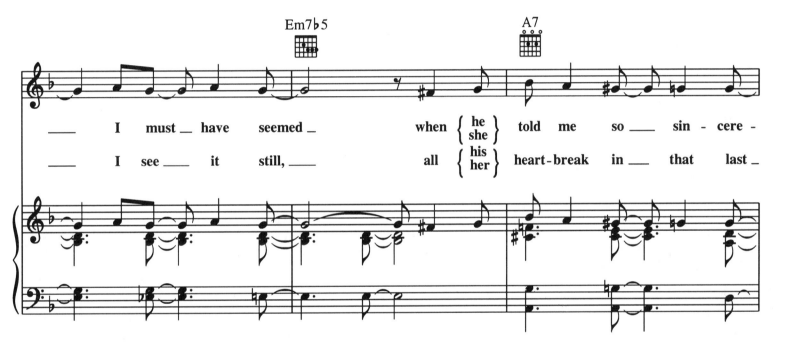

____ I must _ have seemed _ when {he she} told me so ___ sin-cere-
____ I see ___ it still, ___ all {his her} heart-break in ___ that last _

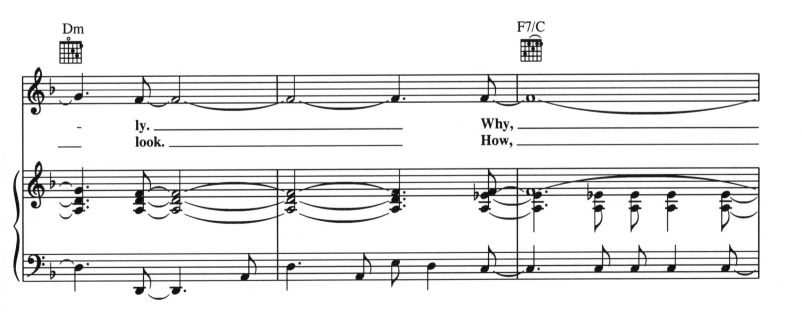

- ly. _____ Why, _____
- look. _____ How, _____

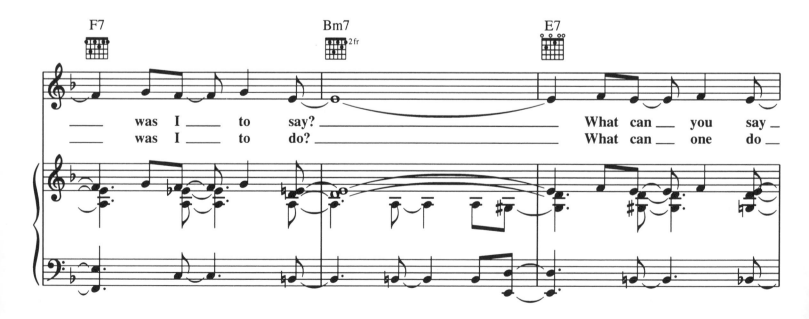

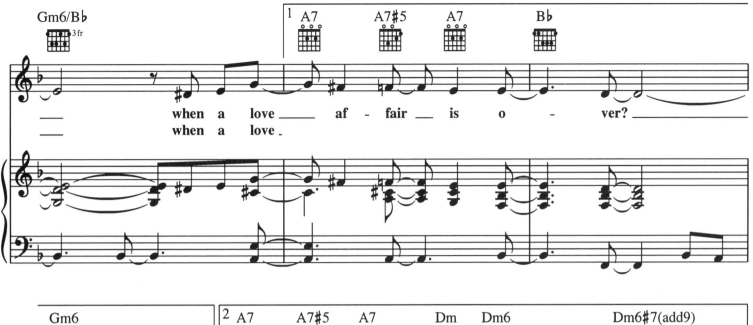

Portuguese Lyrics

A insensatez
Que você fez
Coração mais sem cuidado
Fez chorar de dôr
O seu amôr
Um amôr tão delicado
Ah! Porque você
Foi fraco assim
Assim tão desalmado
Ah! Meu coração
Que nunca amou
Não merece ser amado
Vai meu coração
Ouve a razão
Usa só sinceridade
Quem semeia vento
Diz a razão
Colhe tempestade
Vai meu coração
Pede perdão
Perdão apaixonado
Vai porque
Quem não
Pede perdão
Não é nunca perdoado.

I WILL

Words and Music by JOHN LENNON
and PAUL McCARTNEY

Who knows___ how long___ I've loved___ you?___ You know___ I love___ you still.___
___ I ev - er saw___ you,___ I did - n't catch___ your name,___

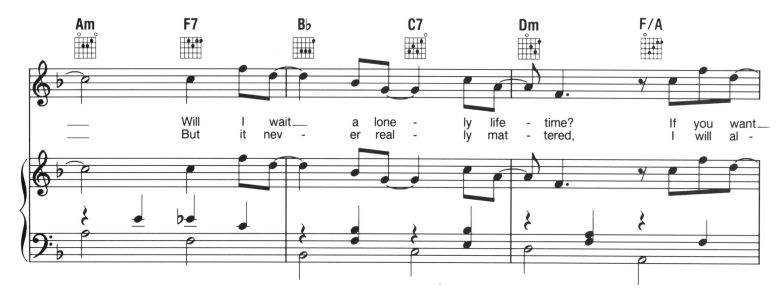

Will I wait___ a lone - ly life - time? If you want
But it nev - er real - ly mat - tered, I will al -

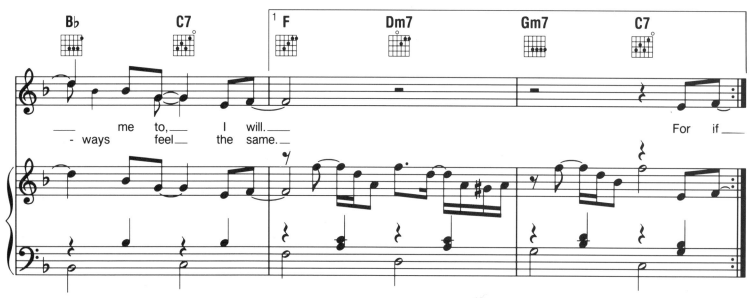

___ me to, I will.
- ways feel___ the same.___

For if___

IF EVER I WOULD LEAVE YOU

from CAMELOT

Words by ALAN JAY LERNER
Music by FREDERICK LOEWE

I WILL FOLLOW HIM
(a/k/a I WILL FOLLOW YOU)

English Lyric by NORMAN GIMBEL and ARTHUR ALTMAN
Original Lyric by JACQUES PLANTE
Music by J.W. STOLE and DEL ROMA

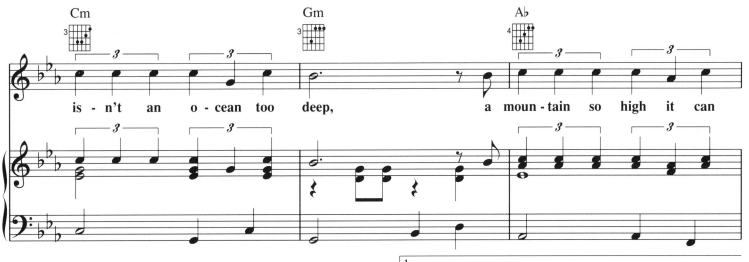

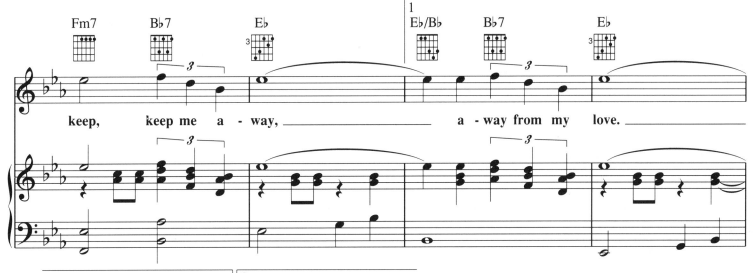

I WILL WAIT FOR YOU
from THE UMBRELLAS OF CHERBOURG

Music by MICHEL LEGRAND
Original French Text by JACQUES DEMY
English Lyrics by NORMAN GIMBEL

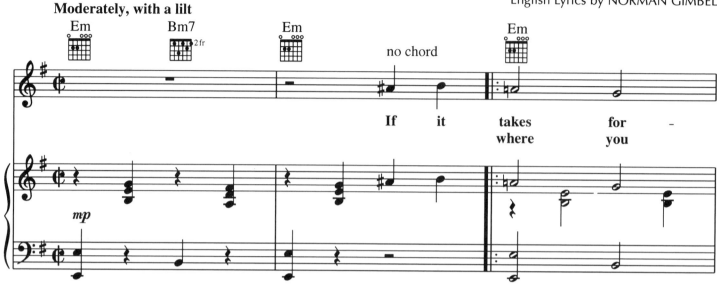

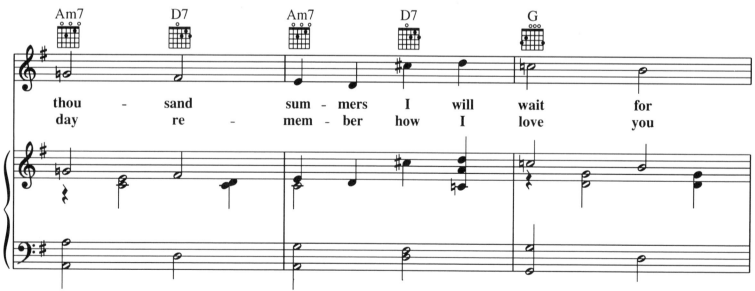

IF YOU GO AWAY

French Words and Music by JACQUES BREL
English Words by ROD McKUEN

Slowly, with much feeling

Chorus

1. If you go a - way on this sum-mer day Then you might as well take the sun a -
(2.) If you go a - way, as I know you will, You must tell the world to stop turn - ing
(3.) If you go a - way, as I know you must, There'll be noth - ing left in the world to

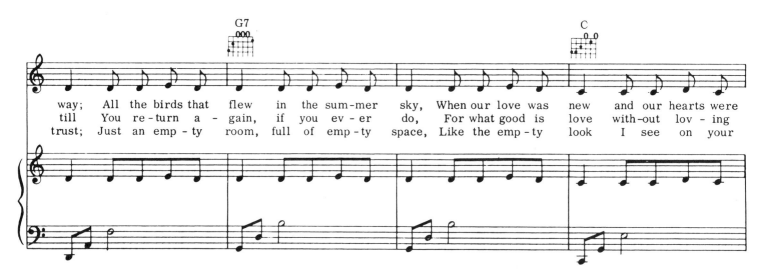

way; All the birds that flew in the sum-mer sky, When our love was new and our hearts were
till You re-turn a - gain, if you ev - er do, For what good is love with-out lov - ing
trust; Just an emp-ty room, full of emp-ty space, Like the emp-ty look I see on your

high; When the day was young_ and the night_ was long, And the moon stood still_ for the night-bird's
you; Can I tell you now,_ as you turn_ to go, I'll be dy - ing slow-ly till the next hel -
face, I'd have been the shad-ow of your shad-ow if I thought it might have kept me by your

IN MY LIFE

Words and Music by JOHN LENNON
and PAUL McCARTNEY

1. plac - es had their mo - ments with lov - ers and friends I
2.3. know I'll nev - er lose af - fec - tion for peo - ple and things that

still can re - call. Some are dead and some are
went be - fore, I know I'll of - ten stop and think a -

B7   Dm   A   To Coda

liv - ing, In my life I've loved them all.
bout them, In my life I love you more.

no chord

8va

in 18th century style

68

LET'S HANG ON

Words and Music by BOB CREWE,
SANDY LINZER and DENNY RANDELL

Additional Lyrics

2. There isn't anything I wouldn't do.
   I'd pay any price to get in good with you.
   Patch it up. (Give me a second turnin'.)
   Patch it up. (Don't cool off while I'm burnin'.)

   You've got me cryin', dyin' at your door.
   Don't shut me out, ooh, let me in once more.
   Open up. (Your arms, I need to hold you.)
   Open up. (Your heart, oh girl, I love you.)

   Baby, don't you know?
   Baby, don't you go.
   Think it over and stay.

LET IT BE ME
(JE T'APPARTIENS)

English Words by MANN CURTIS
French Words by PIERRE DeLANOE
Music by GILBERT BECAUD

Relaxed

I bless the day I found you, I want to stay a-round you,
If, for each day bit of glad - ness, Some - one must taste of sad - ness,

And so I beg you, let it be me. Don't take this
I'll bear the sor - row, let it be me. No mat - ter

heav - en from one, If you must cling to some - one, Now and for - ev - er,
what the price is, I'll make the sac - ri - fic - es, Through each to - mor - row,

THE LOOK OF LOVE

from CASINO ROYALE

Words by HAL DAVID
Music by BURT BACHARACH

Medium Rock Ballad (with much feeling)

The look ___ of love ___ is in ___
of love, ___ it's on ___

your eyes, ___ a look ___ your smile ___
your face, ___ a look ___ that time ___

can't dis - guise. ___ The look ___
can't e - rase. ___ Be mine ___

L-O-V-E

Words and Music by BERT KAEMPFERT
and MILT GABLER

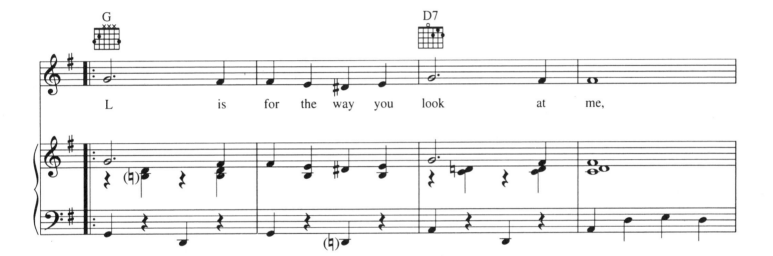

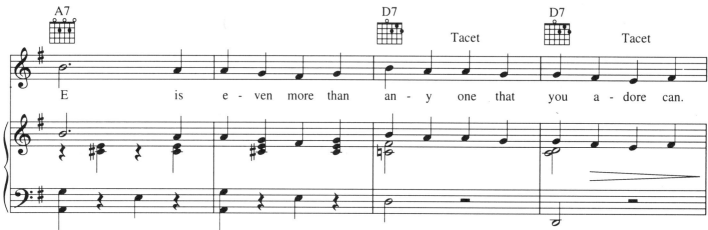

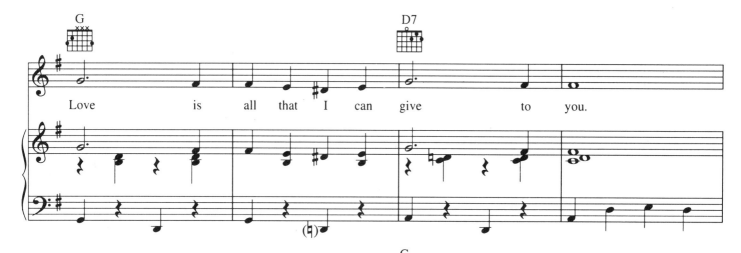

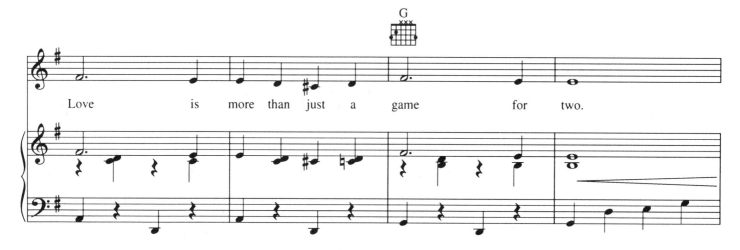

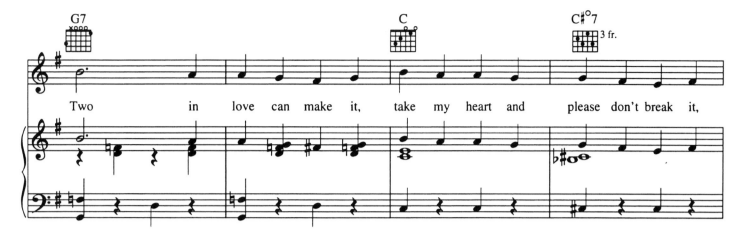

Two   in love can make it, take my heart and   please don't break it,

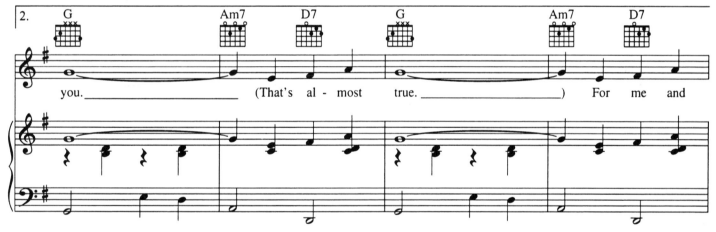

love   was made for me and you._____

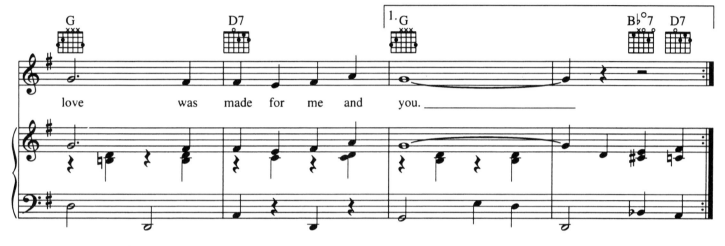

you._____   (That's al - most true._____) For me and

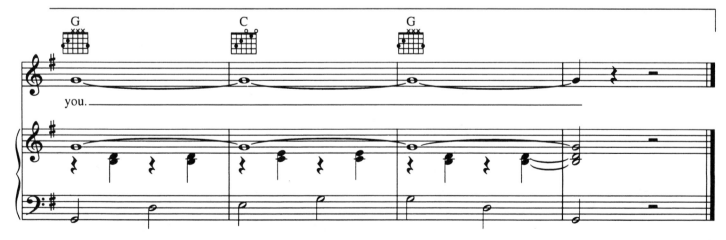

you._____

LOVE
(CAN MAKE YOU HAPPY)

Words and Music by
JACK SIGLER, JR.

Moderately Slow

1. Wake up in the morn - ing, with the
2. If you think you've found some - one you'll

sun - shine in your eyes, __ And the smell of flow - ers
love for - ev - er more, __ then it's worth the

bloom - ing in the air. __ Your
price you'll have to pay, __ pay. __ To

MICHELLE

Words and Music by JOHN LENNON
and PAUL McCARTNEY

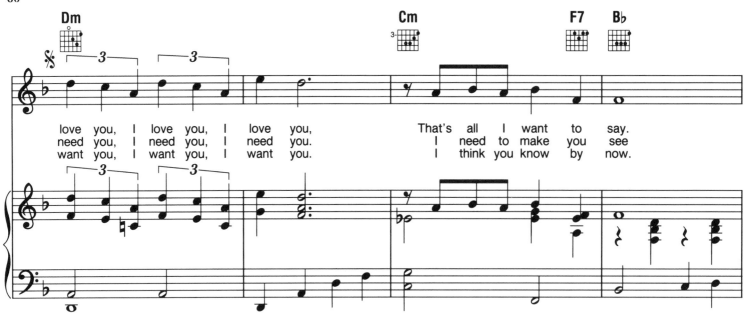

love you, I love you, I love you, That's all I want to say.
need you, I need you, I need you. I need to make you see
want you, I want you, I want you. I think you know by now.

Un - til I find a way _____ I will say the on - ly
what you mean to me. _____ Un - til I do, I'm
I'll get to you some - how. _____ Un - til I do, I'm

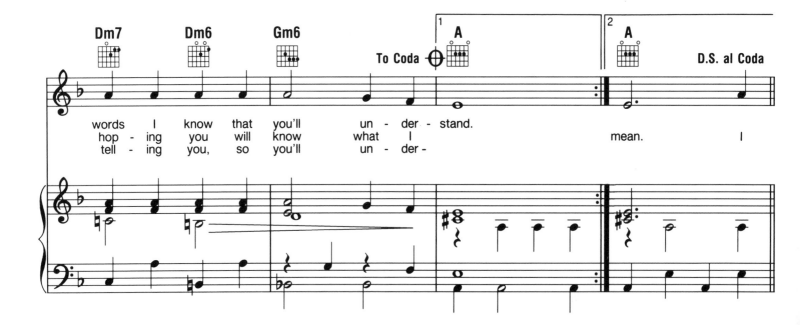

words I know that you'll un - der - stand.
hop - ing you will know what I mean. I
tell - ing you, so you'll un - der -

MORE
Theme from MONDO CANE

English Lyrics by NORMAN NEWELL
Italian Lyrics by M. CIORCIOLINI
Music by NINO OLIVIERO and RIZ ORTOLANI

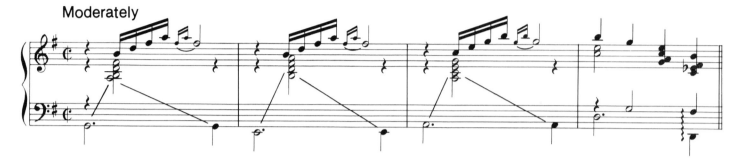

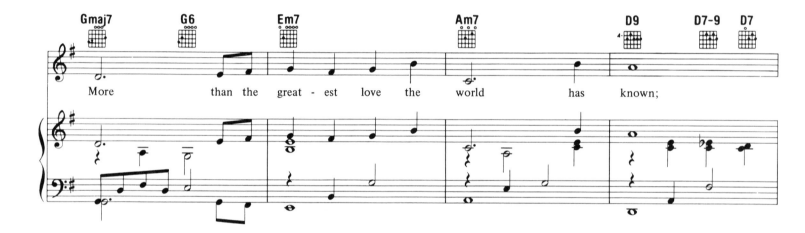

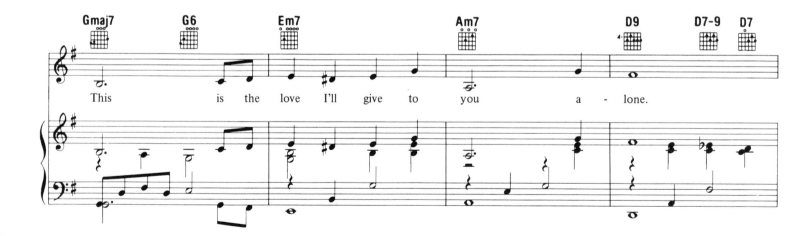

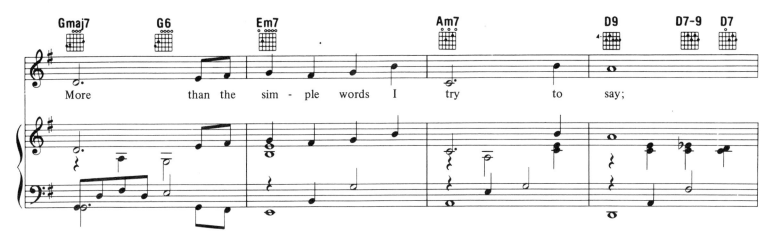

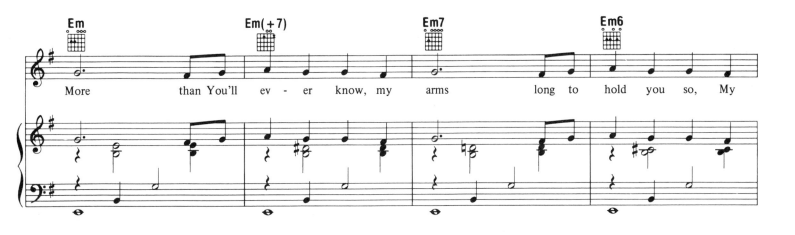

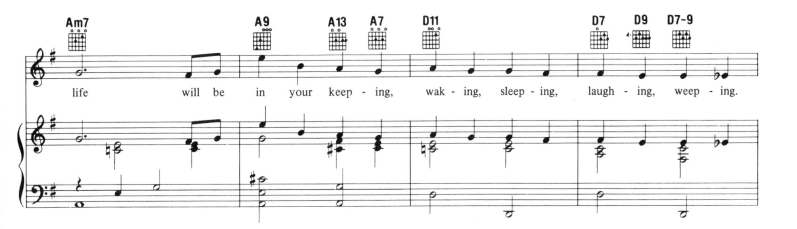

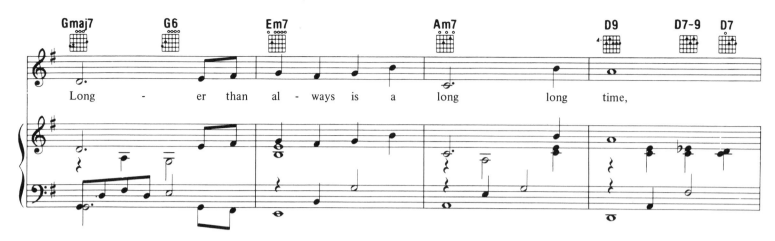

Long - er than al - ways is a long long time,

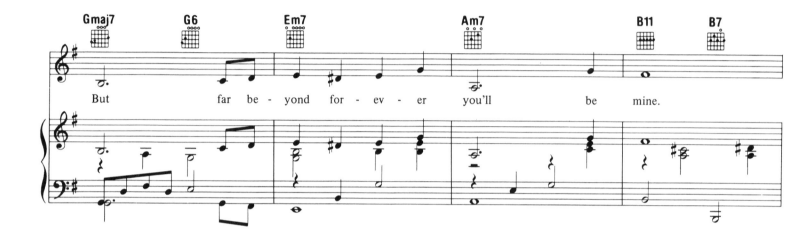

But far be - yond for - ev - er you'll be mine.

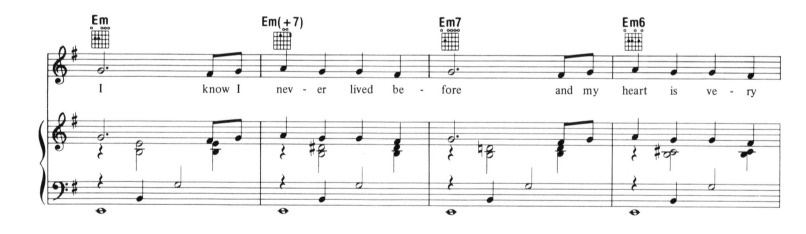

I know I nev - er lived be - fore and my heart is ve - ry

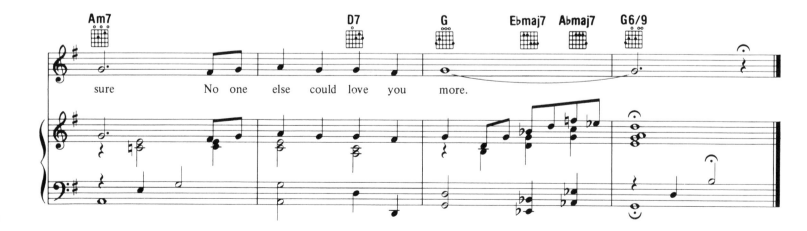

sure No one else could love you more.

MORE TODAY THAN YESTERDAY

Words and Music by
PAT UPTON

MY CUP RUNNETH OVER
from I DO! I DO!

Words by TOM JONES
Music by HARVEY SCHMIDT

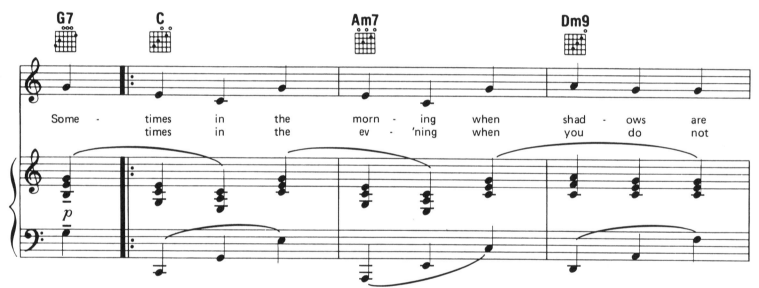

Some - | times in the morn - ing when shad - ows are
times in the ev - 'ning when you do not

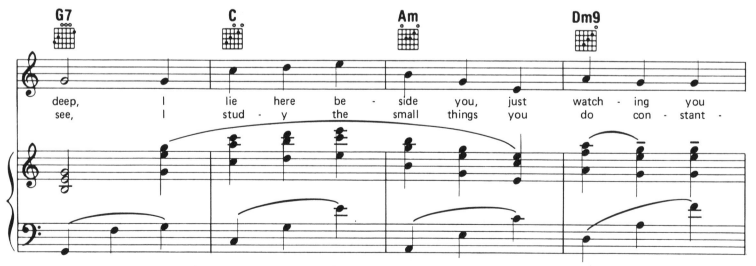

deep, I lie here be - side you, just watch - ing you
see, I stud - y the small things just you do con - stant -

MY LOVE

Words and Music by
TONY HATCH

bright - er than the bright - est __ star that shines ev - 'ry night a - bove __

__ and there is noth - ing in this world that can ev - er change MY

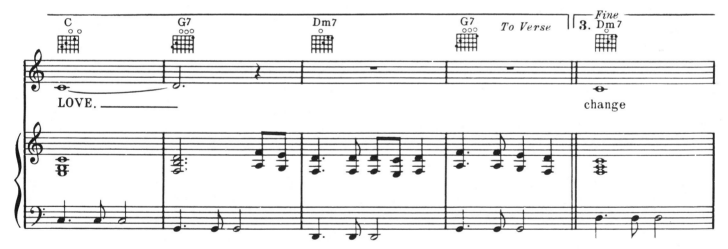

LOVE. _____ change

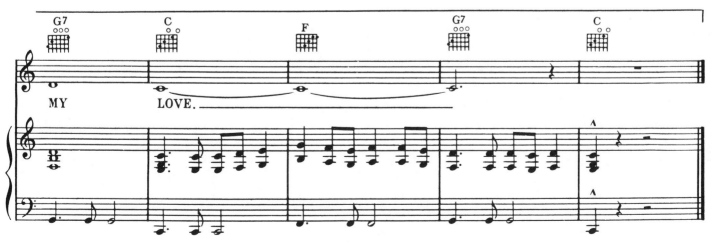

MY LOVE. _____

Verse

Some-thing hap-pened to my heart the day that I met you,
Once I thought that love was meant for an-y-one else but me.

some-thing that I nev-er felt be-fore. _____
Once I thought you'd nev-er come my way. _____

You are al-ways on my mind_ no mat-ter what I do, and
Now it on-ly goes to show_ how wrong we all can be, for

ev-'ry day_ it seems I want you more. _____ MY LOVE is
now I have_ to tell you ev-'ry day. _____

D. S. al Fine

(You Make Me Feel Like)
A NATURAL WOMAN

Words and Music by GERRY GOFFIN,
CAROLE KING and JERRY WEXLER

OUR DAY WILL COME

Words by BOB HILLIARD
Music by MORT GARSON

Slowly, with expression

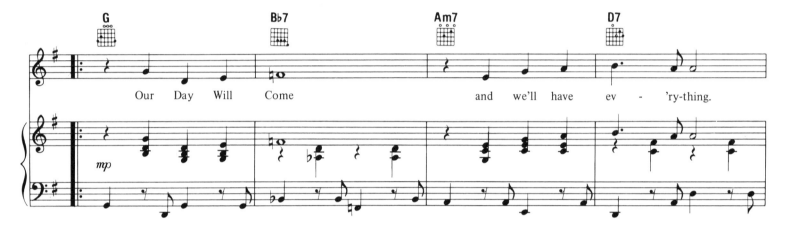

Our Day Will Come and we'll have ev - 'ry-thing.

We'll share the joy fall - ing in love can bring. No one can

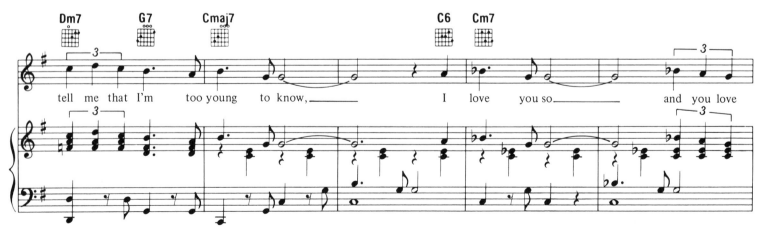

tell me that I'm too young to know, I love you so and you love

MCA music publishing

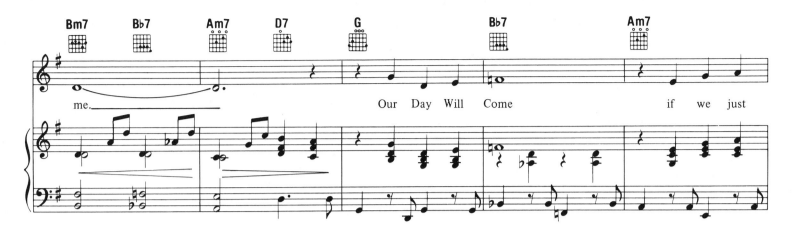

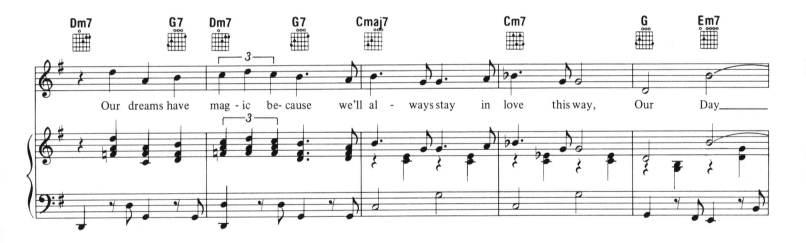

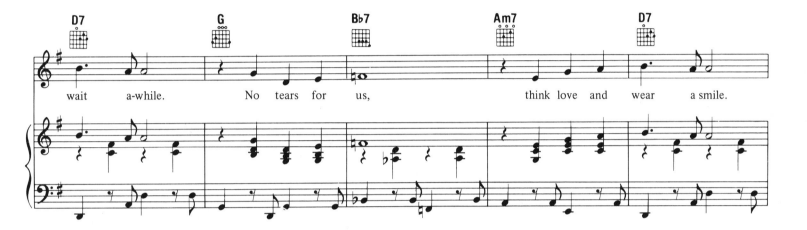

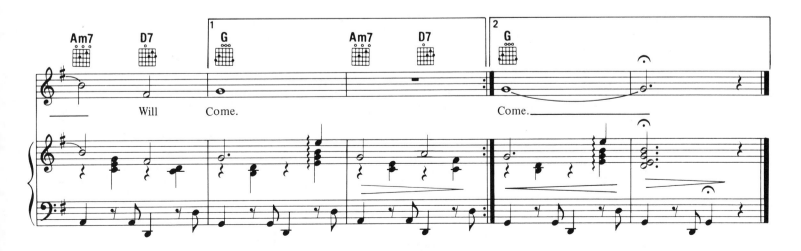

PEOPLE

from FUNNY GIRL

Words by BOB MERRILL
Music by JULE STYNE

P.S. I LOVE YOU

Words and Music by JOHN LENNON
and PAUL McCARTNEY

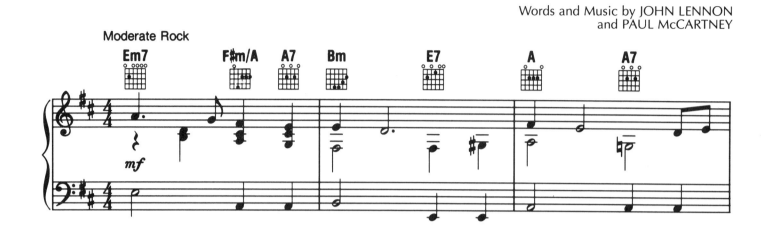

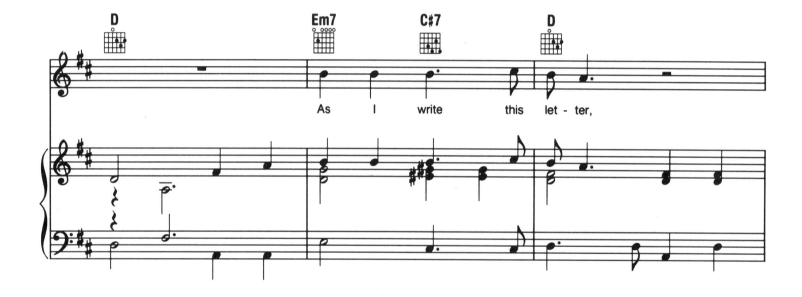

As I write this let-ter,

send my love to you. Re-mem-ber that I'll

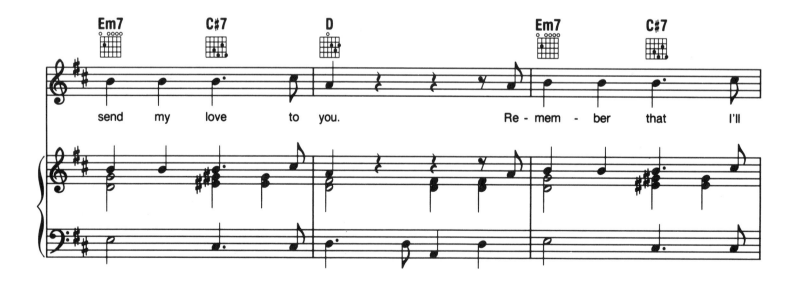

SOMETHING

Words and Music by
GEORGE HARRISON

(YOU'RE MY)
SOUL AND INSPIRATION

Words and Music by BARRY MANN
and CYNTHIA WEIL

Girl, _____ I can't let you do ___ this,
I _____ nev - er had much go - in',

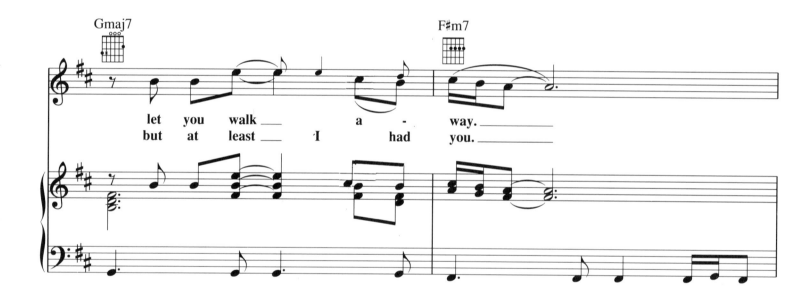

let you walk ___ a - way. _____
but at least ___ I had you. _____

Girl, _____ how can I live through ___ this,
How _____ can you walk out know - in'

STARTING HERE, STARTING NOW

Words and Music by RICHARD MALTBY JR.
and DAVID SHIRE

Quite slowly, with a steady beat

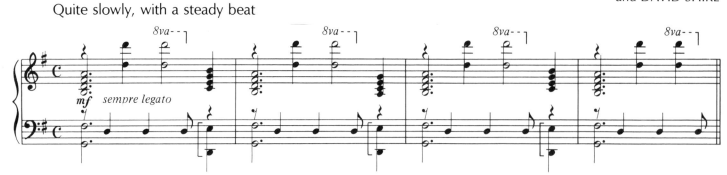

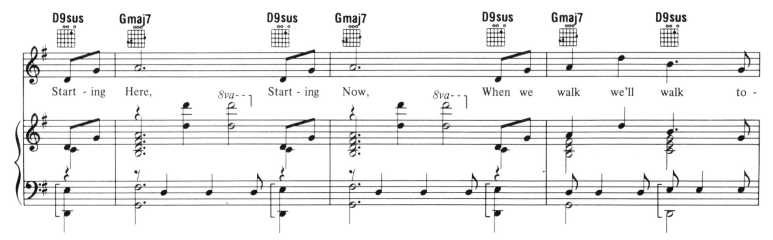

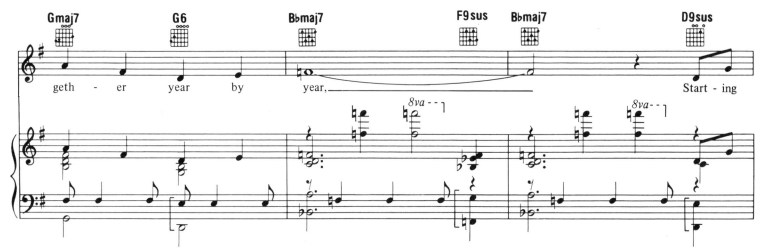

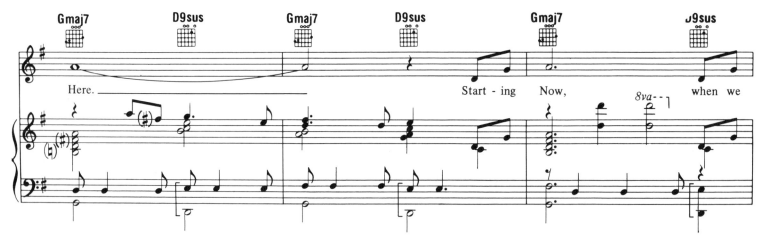

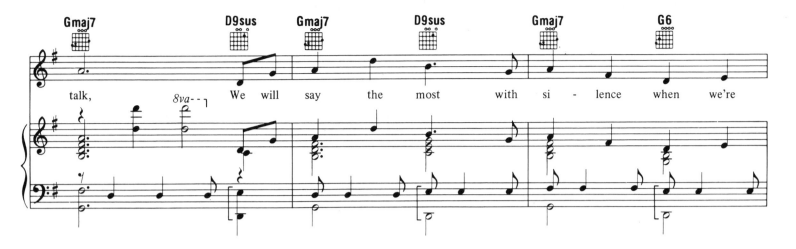

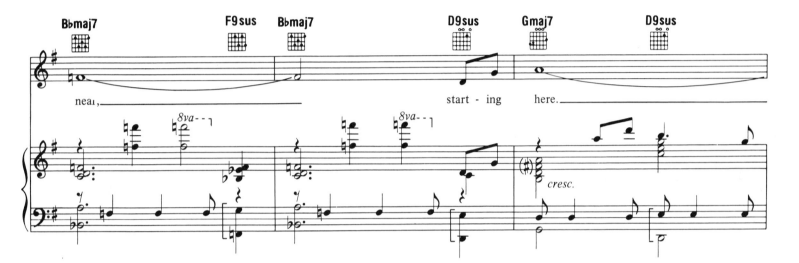

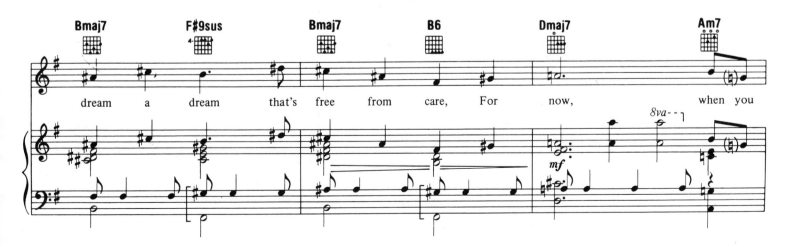

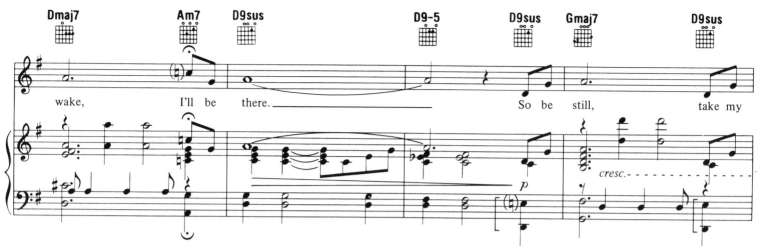

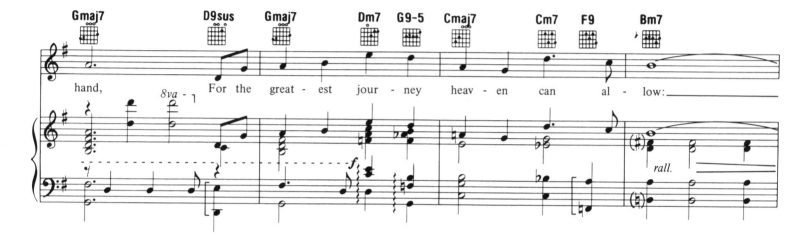

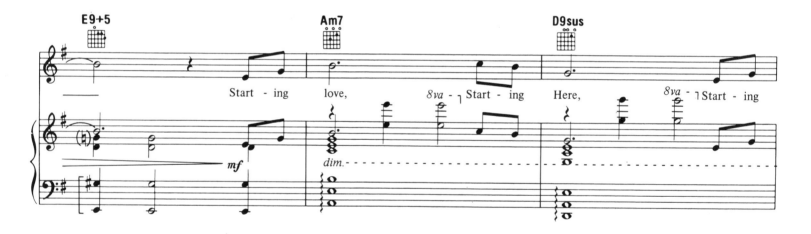

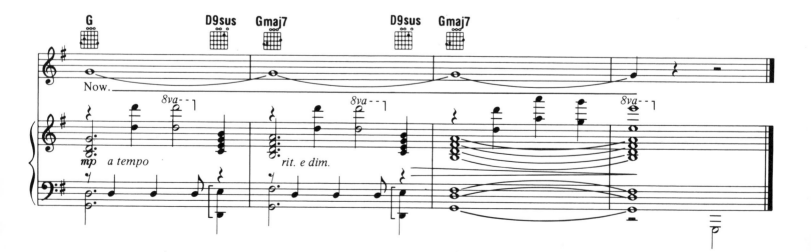

STRANGERS IN THE NIGHT
Adapted from A MAN COULD GET KILLED

Words by CHARLES SINGLETON and EDDIE SNYDER
Music by BERT KAEMPFERT

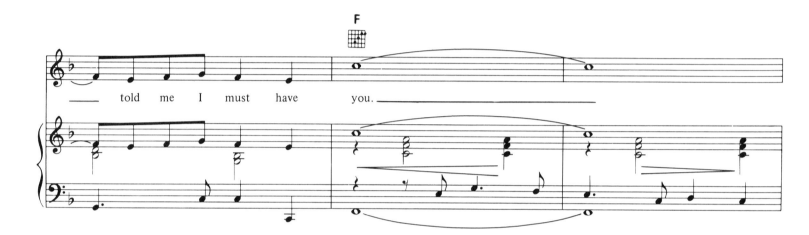

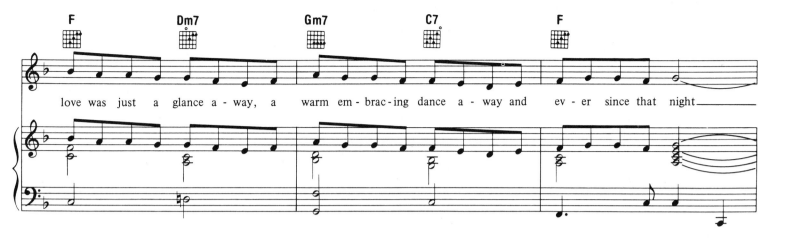

love was just a glance a - way, a warm em - brac - ing dance a - way and ev - er since that night____

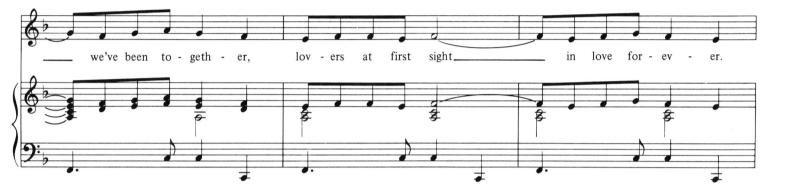

____ we've been to - geth - er, lov - ers at first sight_____ in love for - ev - er.

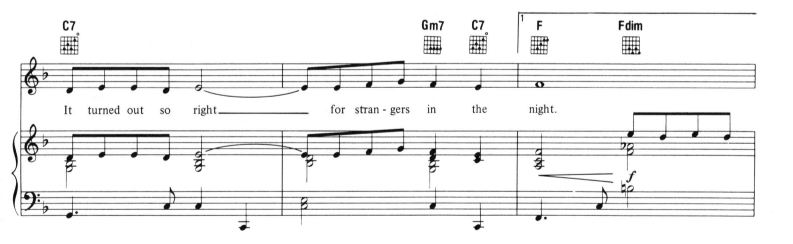

It turned out so right_____ for stran - gers in the night.

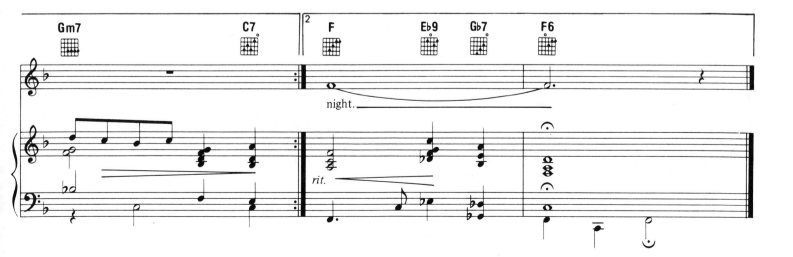

night._____

THERE'S A KIND OF HUSH
(ALL OVER THE WORLD)

Words and Music by LES REED
and GEOFF STEPHENS

Moderately, with a steady beat

There's a kind of hush all o-ver the world to-night, all o-ver the world you can hear the sounds of lov-ers in love.

THIS GUY'S IN LOVE WITH YOU

Lyric by HAL DAVID
Music by BURT BACHARACH

TOGETHER AGAIN

Words and Music by
BUCK OWENS

WEDDING BELL BLUES

Words and Music by
LAURA NYRO

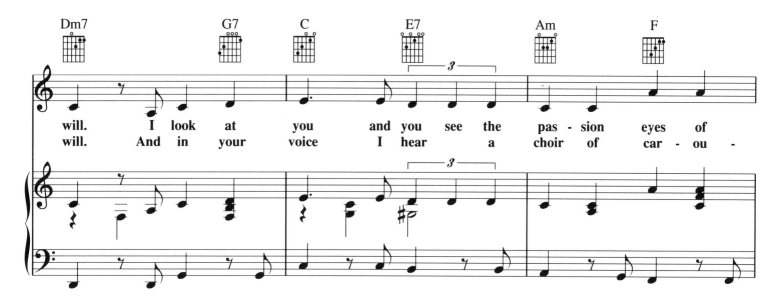

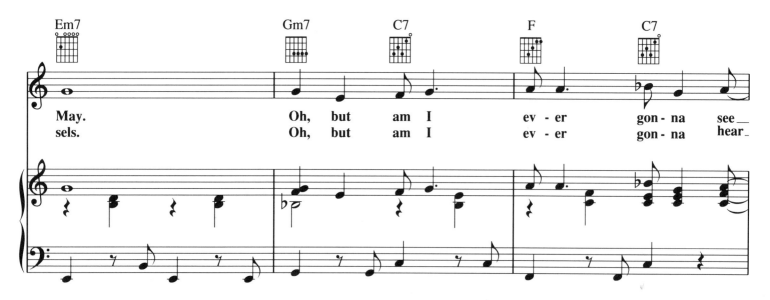

WHAT THE WORLD NEEDS NOW IS LOVE

Lyric by HAL DAVID
Music by BURT BACHARACH

WHEN I'M SIXTY-FOUR

Words and Music by JOHN LENNON
and PAUL McCARTNEY

Moderately

When I get old - er, los - ing my hair___ man - y years from now___

Will you still be send - ing me a val - en - tine,___

WILL YOU LOVE ME TOMORROW
(a/k/a WILL YOU STILL LOVE ME TOMORROW)

Words and Music by GERRY GOFFIN
and CAROLE KING

To-night you're mine com - plete - ly,
Is this a last - ing treas - ure,
I'd like to know that your _____ love

you give your love so
or is just a mo - ment's
is just love I can be

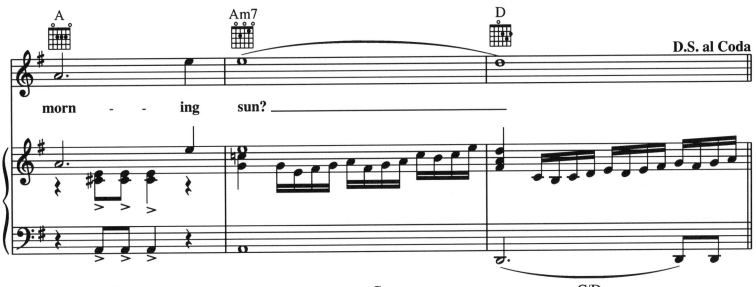

D.S. al Coda

morn - - ing sun? _____

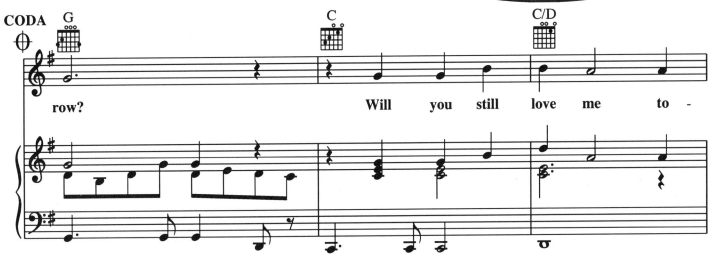

CODA

row?

Will you still love me to -

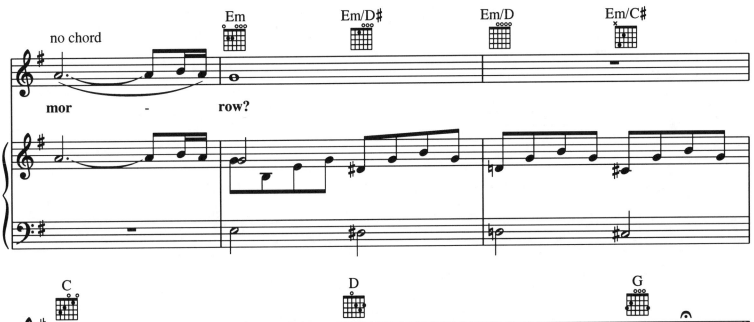

no chord

mor - row?

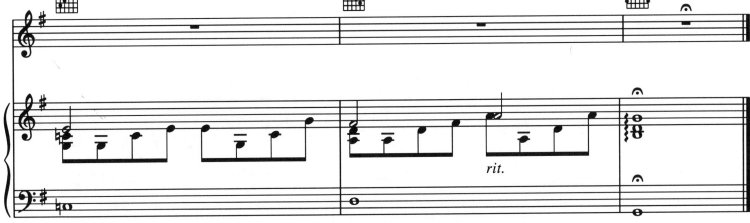

rit.

A TIME FOR US
(LOVE THEME)
from the Paramount Picture ROMEO AND JULIET

Words by LARRY KUSIK and EDDIE SNYDER
Music by NINO ROTA